聖誕村籠罩在雪白之中,村民們期待著亮燈儀式。

sing3 daan3 cyun1 lung4 zaau3 zoi6 syut3 baak6 zi1 zung1,cyun1 man4 mun4 kei4 doi6 zyu3 loeng6 dang1 ji4 sik1。

daan6 si6，gam1 nin4 dik1 mo1 faat3
sing1 sing1 bat1 gin3 liu5！

但是，今年的魔法星星不見了！

But this year, the magical star was missing!

ngo5 mun4 jiu3 zaau2 dou3 sing1 sing1！ siu2 gin1 gwo2 deoi3 siu2 luk6 luk6 syut3

「我們要找到星星！」小堅果對小鹿鹿說。

"We have to find the star!"
Nutty said to Dottie.

taa1 mun4 ceon4 zyu3 mei4 joek6 dik1 gwong1 mong4 zau2 zeon3 sam1 lam4 。

他們循著微弱的光芒走進森林。

taa1 mun4 ceon4 zyu3 mei4 joek6 dik1 gwong1 mong4 zau2 zeon3 sam1 lam4。

光芒帶他們來到了一個冰雪洞穴。

The glow led them to an icy cave.

zoi6 dung6 jyut6 leoi5, taa1 mun4 faat3 jin6
liu5 jat1 zek3 syut3 tou3.

在洞穴裡，他們發現了一隻雪兔。

Inside the cave, they found a snow rabbit.

syut3 tou3 pou5 zoek3 mo1 faat3 sing1 sing1, ngaan5 san4 daai3 zoek3 jat1 si1 oi1 soeng1.

雪兔抱著魔法星星，眼神帶著一絲哀傷。

The snow rabbit was holding the magical star, its eyes full of sadness.

sing1 sing1 si6 ngo5 dik1, ceng2 bat1 jiu3 naa4 zau2 taa1. syut3 tou3 heng1 seng1 syut3.

「星星是我的，請不要拿走它。」雪兔輕聲說。

"The star is mine, please don't take it away," said the snow rabbit softly.

wai6 sam6 mo1 nei5 seoi1 jiu3 sing1 sing1 ne1? siu2 gin1 go2 man6.

「為什麼你需要星星呢?」小堅果問。

"Why do you need the star?" Nutty asked.

syut3 tou3 dai1 haa6 tau4 syut3：「ngo5 mut6 jau5 pang4 jau5, sing1 sing1 joeng6 ngo5 bat1 zoi3 naa5 mo1 laang5 cing1.」

雪兔低下頭說：「我沒有朋友，星星讓我不再那麼冷清。」

The snow rabbit lowered its head and said, "I don't have friends. The star makes me feel less lonely."

siu2 luk2 luk2 wan1 jau4 dei6 syut3 :「ngo5 mun4 ho2 ji5 dong1 nei5 dik1 pang4 jau5 aa1/aa3!」

小鹿鹿溫柔地說:「我們可以當你的朋友啊!」

"We can be your friends!" said Dottie gently.

syut3 tou3 dik1 ji5 doe2 syu6 liu5 hei2 loi4：「zan1 dik1 maa3?」

雪兔的耳朵豎了起來：「真的嗎？」

The snow rabbit's ears perked up. "Really?"

siu2 gin1 go2 siu3 zoek3 syut3:「dong1 jin4 laa1! bat1 gwo3 ngo5 mun4 jaa5 seoi1 jiu3 sing1 sing1 loi4 dim2 loeng6 cyun1 zong1.」

小堅果笑著說:「當然啦!不過我們也需要星星來點亮村莊。」

Nutty smiled and said, "Of course! But we also need the star to light up the village."

syut3 tou3 jau4 jyu6 liu5 jat1 haa5, zeoi3 hau6 baa2
sing1 sing1 dai6 kap1 taa1 mun4.

雪兔猶豫了一下，最後把星星遞給他們。

The snow rabbit hesitated, then handed them the star.

「當然可以!」小鹿鹿開心地回答。
"Of course you can!" Dottie said happily.

「可以帶我一起去嗎？」雪兔小聲問。
"Can I come with you?" the snow rabbit asked softly.

taa1 mun4 jat1 hei2 wui4 dou3 cyun1 zong1, baa2 sing1
sing1 fong3 wui4 sing3 daan3 syu6 deng2.

他們一起回到村莊，把星星放回聖誕樹頂。

Together, they returned to the village and placed the star back on the tree.

**sing3 daan3 syu6 dik1 gwong1 mong4 ziu3
loeng6 liu5 zing2 go3 cyun1 zong1.**

聖誕樹的光芒照亮了整個村莊。

The Christmas tree's light brightened the entire village.

syut3 tou3 dai6 jat1 ci3 gam2 sau6 dou2 pang4
jau5 daai3 loi4 dik1 wan1 nyun5.

雪兔第一次感受到朋友帶來的溫暖。

For the first time, the snow rabbit felt the warmth of friendship.

"Merry Christmas!" Nutty, Dottie, and the snow rabbit shouted together.

「sing3 daan3 faai3 lok6!」
siu2 gin1 go2, siu2 luk2 luk2 wo4 syut3
tou3 jat1 hei2 haam3 dou6.

「聖誕快樂!」
小堅果、小鹿鹿和雪兔一起喊道。

www.ingramcontent.com/pod-product-compliance
Lightning Source LLC
Chambersburg PA
CBHW041704160426